RISK ASSESSMENT

A Gower Health and Safety Workbook

Graham Roberts-Phelps

Gower

Published by
Gower Publishing Limited
Gower House
Croft Road
Aldershot
Hampshire GU11 3HR
England

Gower
Old Post Road
Brookfield
Vermont 05036
USA

Reprinted 2000

Graham Roberts-Phelps has asserted his right under the Copyright, Designs and Patents Act 1988 to be identified as the author of this work.

British Library Cataloguing in Publication Data
Roberts-Phelps, Graham
    Risk assessment. – (A Gower health and safety workbook)
    1.Risk assessment 2.Industrial safety 3.Safety regulations
    I.Title
    363.1'02

ISBN 0 566 08066 4

Typeset in Times by Wearset, Boldon, Tyne and Wear and printed in Great Britain by print in black, Midsomer Norton.

Contents

Chapter 1
Introduction

This first chapter acts as a record of your progress through the workbook and provides a place to summarize your notes and ideas on applying or implementing any of the points covered.

PERSONAL DETAILS

Name:	
Position:	
Location:	
Date started:	Date completed:

Chapter title	Signed	Date
1. Introduction		
2. Understanding safety legislation		
3. Understanding safety in the workplace		
4. Practical risk assessment		
5. Learning review		
6. Risk assessment checklists		
Demonstration of safety in the workplace		
Steps taken to reduce risks and hazards		

Safety review dates	Assessed by	Date
1 month	_____	_____
2 months	_____	_____
3 months	_____	_____
6 months	_____	_____

HOW TO USE THIS SELF-STUDY WORKBOOK

Overview

This self-study workbook is designed to be either one, or a combination, of the following:

◆ a self-study workbook to be completed during working hours in the student's normal place of work, with a review by a trainer, manager or safety officer at a later date

◆ a training programme workbook that can be either fully or partly completed during a training event or events, with the uncompleted sections finished in the student's normal working hours away from the training room.

It contains six self-contained chapters which should each take about 20 minutes to complete, with Chapter 5, 'Learning Review', taking slightly longer due to the testing and validation instruments. Chapter 6 comprises ten simple, general checklists which can be used as an aid in making workplace risk assessments.

It is essential that students discuss their notes and answers from all sections with a supervisor, trainer or coach.

NOTES FOR TRAINERS AND MANAGERS

For use in a training session

If you are using the workbook in a training event you might choose to send the manual to students in advance of their attendance, asking them to complete the Introduction (Chapter 1). Other exercises can then be utilized as required during the programme.

For use as an open-learning or self-study tool

Make sure that you have read the workbook properly yourself and know what the answers are. Anticipate any areas where students may require further support or clarification.

Comprehension testing

Each section features one or more summary exercises to aid understanding and test retention. Chapter 5, 'Learning Review', contains a set of tests, case studies and exercises that test application and knowledge. Suggested answers to these are given in the Appendix.

If you are sending the workbook out to trainees, it is advisable to send an accompanying note reproducing, or drawing attention to, the points contained in the section 'Notes for Students'. Also, be sure to set a time deadline for completing the workbook, perhaps setting a review date in advance.

The tests contained in the learning review can be marked and scored as a percentage if required. You might choose to set a 'pass' or 'fail' standard for completion of the workbook, with certification for all those attaining a suitable standard. Trainees who do not reach the required grade on first completion might then be further coached and have points discussed on an individual basis.

NOTES FOR STUDENTS

This self-study workbook is designed to help you better understand and apply the topic of risk assessment. It may be used either as part of a training programme, or for self-study at your normal place of work, or as a combination of both.

Here are some guidelines on how to gain the most from this workbook.

- ◆ Find 20 minutes during which you will not be disturbed.

- ◆ Read, complete and review one chapter at a time.

- ◆ Do not rush any chapter or exercise – time taken now will pay dividends later.

- ◆ Complete each written exercise as fully as you can.

- ◆ Make notes of questions or points that come to mind when reading through the sections.

- ◆ Discuss anything that you do not understand with your manager, safety officer or work colleagues.

Chapter 5, 'Learning Review', is a scored test that may carry a pass or fail mark.

At regular intervals throughout the workbook there are exercises to complete and opportunities to make notes on any topics or points that you feel are particularly important or relevant to you. These are marked as:

Notes

_____

_____

_____

_____

LEARNING DIARY

Personal Learning Diary

Name: _____

Job Title: _____

Company: _____

Date: _____

The value of the training programme will be greatly enhanced if you complete and review the following Learning Diary before, during and after reviewing and reading the workbook.

LEARNING OBJECTIVES

At the start or before completing the workbook, please take time to consider what you would like to learn or be able to do better as a result of the training process. Please be as specific as possible, relating points directly to the requirements of your job or work situation. If possible, please involve your manager, supervisor or team leader in agreeing these objectives.

Record these objectives below

1.

2.

3.

4.

5.

6.

> **PLEASE COMPLETE**
> **BEFORE CONTINUING**

LEARNING LOG

During the training programme there will be many useful ideas and learning points that you will want to apply in the workplace.

Key ideas/learning points	How I will apply these at work

> **PLEASE COMPLETE**
> **BEFORE CONTINUING**

LEARNING APPLICATION

As you complete each chapter, please consider and identify the specific opportunities for applying the skills, knowledge, behaviours and attitudes and record these below.

Action planned, with dates	Review/comments

Remember, it may take time and practice to achieve new results.
Review these goals periodically and discuss with your manager.

PLEASE COMPLETE
BEFORE CONTINUING

HOW TO GET THE BEST RESULTS FROM THIS WORKBOOK

The format of this workbook is interactive; it requires you to complete various written exercises. This aids both learning retention and comprehension and, most importantly, acts as a permanent record of completion and learning. It is therefore essential that you **complete all exercises, assignments and questions**.

In order to gain the maximum value and benefit from the time that you invest in completing this workbook, use the following guidelines.

Pace yourself

You might choose to work through the whole workbook in one session or, alternatively, you might find it easier to take one chapter at a time. This is the recommended approach. If you are using this workbook as part of a live training programme, then make time to follow through any unfinished exercises or topics afterwards.

Share your own opinions and experience

We all have a different view of the world, and we all have different backgrounds and experiences. As you complete the workbook it is essential that you relate the learning points directly to your own situation, beliefs and work environment.

Please complete the exercises using relevant examples that are personal and specific to you.

Keep an open mind

Some of the material you will be covering may be simple common sense, and some of it will be familiar to you. Other ideas may not be so familiar, so it pays to keep an open mind, as most learning involves some form of change. This may take the form of changing your ideas, changing an attitude, changing your perception of what is true, or changing your behaviours and the way you do things.

When we experience change, in almost anything, our first automatic reaction is resistance, but this is not usually the most useful response. Remember, safety is something we have been aware of for a long time, and consider (or fail to consider, as the case may be!) every day. As a result, we follow procedures without thinking – on auto-pilot as it were. This often means that we have a number of bad habits of which we are unaware.

Example of change:

Sign your name here as you would normally do:

*Now hold the pen or pencil in the **opposite** hand to that which you normally use and sign your name again:*

Apart from noting how difficult this might have been, consider also how 'strange' and uncomfortable this seemed. You could easily learn to sign your name with either hand, usually far more quickly than you might think. However the resistance to change may take longer to overcome.

Make   Notes

Making notes not only gives you information to refer to later, perhaps while reviewing the workbook, but it also aids memory. Many people find that making notes actually helps them to remember things more accurately and for longer. So, as you come across points that are particularly useful or of particular interest, please take a couple of moments to write these down, underline them or make comments in the margin or spaces provided.

Review with others

In particular, ask questions and discuss your answers and thoughts with your colleagues and fellow managers, especially points which you are not sure of, points which you are not quite clear on, and perhaps points about which you would like to understand more.

Before you start any of the main chapters, please complete the following learning assignments.

Learning Objectives

It is often said that if you do not know where you are going, any road will get you there. To put it another way, it is difficult to hit the target you cannot see. To gain the most benefit from this workbook, it is best to have some objectives.

Overall objectives

- **Improvements.** We don't have to be ill to improve our fitness. Improvement is always possible.

- **Skills.** Learn new skills, tips and techniques.

- **Knowledge.** Gain a better understanding of safety issues.

- **Attitudes.** Change the way we think about safety issues.

- **Changes.** Change specific attitudes on behaviours and our safety procedures and practice.

- **Ideas.** Share ideas.

Here are some areas in which you can apply your overall objectives.

1. Hazards and risks

The first objective is to be able to identify safety hazards and risks. These may exist all around us and may not be readily identifiable as such – for example, the ordinary moving of boxes or small items, using a kettle or hand drill, cleaning and so on.

2. Prevention

Prevention is always better than cure, and part of this workbook will deal with knowing how to prevent accidents and injuries in the first place. Injuries are nearly always painful both in human and business terms. As well as accidents that cause us or others harm, there are many more accidents that cause damage and cost money to put right.

3. Understanding your safety responsibilities

Health and safety is everybody's responsibility, and safety is a full-time job. As you complete this workbook you will be looking at how it affects you personally and the role that you can play, not only for your own safety but also for the safety of others around you.

4. Identifying ways to make your workplace safer

A workbook like this also gives us the opportunity to put ideas together on how we can improve the health and safety environment of our workplace. We do not have to have safety problems in order to improve safety, any more than we have to be ill to become fitter.

An improvement in working conditions does not have to cost much or be very complicated. Simply moving a filing cabinet to a more convenient location can often represent a quantum leap in working safely.

Make a note here of any personal objectives that you may have.

Notes

_____

_____

_____

_____

_____

_____

OPINION POLL

Consider the following statements, first marking each with your level of agreement, and then making some supporting comments regarding these views.

5 = Strongly agree; 4 = Agree; 3 = Neither agree nor disagree; 2 = Disagree; 1 = Strongly disagree.

1. Every accident or injury can be prevented or avoided.

Circle one response: 5 4 3 2 1

Comments:

2. Every accident or work-related injury or discomfort is caused by human error in some way.

Circle one response: 5 4 3 2 1

Comments:

3. You cannot motivate people to be safer; you can only enforce rules and penalties.

Circle one response: 5 4 3 2 1

Comments:

4. Left to their own devices, people and organizations will take unnecessary risks and cut corners.

Circle one response: 5 4 3 2 1

Comments:

PLEASE COMPLETE
BEFORE CONTINUING

OPINION POLL: REVIEW

1. Every accident or injury can be prevented or avoided.

This is largely held to be true. Research shows that nearly all accidents are a result of a cause and effect relationship. If you identify the causes, you can change the effects.

2. Every accident or work-related injury or discomfort is caused by human error in some way.

As a computer programmer once remarked, 'There is no such thing as "computer error", only incorrect user input'. 'Accidents' are caused by people and their behaviours, not by machines, chemicals or inanimate objects.

3. You cannot motivate people to be safer; you can only enforce rules and penalties.

Hopefully, people will work safely and consider their own welfare and that of others without legal or management interference, although statistics do not prove this to be the case. In countries without enforced legislation, people are made to endure terrible work environments with little or no regard for safety. Consider how many of us wear a seat belt today compared with the number who did so before it became law.

4. Left to their own devices people and organizations will take unnecessary risks and cut corners.

Accident investigators and HSE inspectors have thousands of examples which prove this statement to be true. You cannot have a quality company that does not consider the health and safety of its staff and customers as the highest priority.

Chapter 2
Understanding
Safety Legislation

This chapter examines the current regulations and standards of safe working practice.

Before starting this chapter, please take a few moments to make a note of any ideas or actions in the learning diary and log in Chapter 1.

The biggest risk is not taking safety seriously.

MAKING SAFETY A PRIORITY

Under the Health and Safety at Work Act 1974 (HASAWA) you have to ensure the health and safety of yourself and others who may be affected by what you do or fail to do. This means making health and safety a priority.

This includes people who work for you (including casual workers, part-timers, trainees and sub-contractors), use workplaces which you provide, are allowed to use your equipment, visit your premises, may be affected by your work, (for example, your neighbours or the public), use products that you make, supply or import, or use your professional services (for example, if you are a designer).

The Act applies to all work activities and premises and everyone at work has responsibilities under it, including the self-employed.

New regulations have replaced and updated much of the old law on Health and Safety, but there are specific laws applying to certain premises, such as the Factories Act 1961 and the Offices, Shops and Railway Premises Act 1963.

Consider these points:

♦ The same mistakes that cause injury and cost lives can also damage property, equipment, delay production and inconvenience customers.

♦ There are no such things as 'minimal acceptable level' – **all** accidents must be controlled and prevented.

♦ A quality company is a **safe** company.

Make a note of any important points arising from this section.

Notes

_____

_____

_____

_____

SAFETY IN THE WORKPLACE

Common law requires that an employer must take reasonable care to protect his employees from risk of foreseeable injury, disease or death at work. In the nineteenth and twentieth centuries employers argued with reasonable success against this duty. It was not until 1938 that the House of Lords identified, in general terms, the duties of employers at common law.

Whilst it is obviously good common sense to work safely, minimizing the chances of accidents, it is also a point of law. There are two main kinds of Health and Safety law. Some is very specific about what you must do, and some is much more general, applying to almost every business. In this short summary we will be looking at the key legislation that affects your work, and translating it into practical measures by which we must all abide.

Never underestimate the consequences of breaking Health and Safety legislation. We can all remember terrible accidents such as the Zeebrugge disaster or the Clapham rail accident. However, there are many hundreds of thousands of accidents each year that do not make the headlines but still ruin lives and businesses.

Legally, accidents like these can cost companies and individuals thousands and sometimes hundreds of thousands of pounds.

> **Example:** *A meat processing plant was burnt to the ground by a fault caused during work on a piece of machinery. The fire alarm and fire sprinklers failed to operate properly – both legal requirements. Fortunately nobody was badly hurt.*
>
> *Any fines imposed by the courts would be insignificant compared to the loss of business, customer contracts, and the effects on 100 employees who lost their jobs for a year while the factory was rebuilt.*

Some risks are very obvious; others less so. The purpose of legislation is that all possible steps are taken to eliminate hazards, reduce risks, and inform and implement safe systems of work.

25% of all fatal accidents, and many more serious injuries, are caused because safe systems of work are not provided for, or even ignored.

Safety law: what does it mean to you?

Safety regulations or legislation creates very real obligations not only on companies and organizations, but also on the directors, managers and individual employees. Whilst some are over 20 years old, many are much more recent and it is important that we are fully aware of the consequences and the requirements of each set of regulations. As the law says, ignorance is no defence.

If there is an accident, Health and Safety law is interpreted so that the company or organization has to prove that it was not at fault. In other words, it is assumed that the organization has not met its Health and Safety obligations, unless it can prove otherwise. Therefore, failure to comply in a way that demonstrates and proves that legislation has been adhered to can easily lead to prosecution resulting in fines and, in some cases, imprisonment.

Some legislation that may affect you

- Health and Safety at Work Act 1974

- Electricity at Work Regulations 1989

- COSHH Regulations 1994

- Manual Handling Operations Regulations 1992

- Noise at Work Regulations 1989

- Fire Precautions Act 1971

- Display Screen Equipment Regulations 1992

- Workplace (Health, Safety and Welfare) Regulations 1992

- Management of Health and Safety at Work Regulations 1992 ·J MHSW·

- Provision and Use of Work Equipment Regulations 1992

- Safety Signs and Signals Regulations 1996

- RIDDOR 1995

- Consultation with Employees Regulations 1996

In law, ignorance is no defence.

Make a note of any points from this section that concern you.

Notes

_____

_____

_____

_____

_____

_____

_____

HEALTH AND SAFETY AT WORK ACT 1974

This is the main law that covers **everyone** at work and **all work premises**.

> *It simply means making sure that people work safely, are safe and that their welfare is not put at risk.*

Enacted in 1974, this piece of legislation was brought in to replace and update much of the old Health and Safety law that was contained in the Factories Act 1961 and the Offices, Shops and Railway Premises Act 1963. These two laws were rapidly becoming out-of-date with the advent of modern working practices, technology and equipment.

Under the Health and Safety at Work Act (HASAWA) a company has to ensure the health and safety of all its employees. Individuals have to ensure the health and safety of themselves and others around them who may be affected by what they do or fail to do. This includes contractors, as well as customers or, indeed, anyone who may come into contact with the organization.

> *Safety studies have highlighted that small firms (those with fewer than 50 employees) have poorer accident records than large organizations. This is made even worse by the large number of accidents that go unreported by small companies. Ignorance, poor standards and contempt for basic safety standards have been highlighted as key contributing factors.*

The Act applies to all work activities and premises, and everyone at work has responsibilities under it – including the self-employed. Here are some key points raised by the Act.

1. Safeguards

Employers are required to implement reasonable safeguards to ensure safe working practice at all times. This means taking every practical step to remove hazards and reduce or eliminate risks. The law interprets this as taking every possible precaution, and cost is not considered as an excuse for failure to do this.

2. Written policy

All organizations employing five or more people must have a written and up-to-date health and safety policy. In addition, they must carry out written risk assessments as part of the implementation of their safety policy and also display a current certificate as required by the Employer's Liability (Compulsory Insurance) Act 1969.

3. Training and information

Following on from this, all staff must be fully trained, equipped and informed of not only the company's safety policy and procedures, but also of the skills and knowledge necessary to carry out their normal work duties. This, of course, means displaying Health and Safety regulations and safety signs, as well as formally training and directing staff on all aspects of health, safety, hazards and risks.

4. Reasonable care

The legislation does not just cover employers and organizations; there are definite requirements placed on employees. All employees must take reasonable care not only to protect themselves, but also their colleagues. They are also required to follow all health and safety policy regulations and procedures in full and to cooperate fully with health and safety representatives and officers in their job of implementing Health and Safety policies. Failure to do so is in breach of the Act.

HSE inspectors can visit without notice and have right of entry. They have the power to stop your work, close premises and even prosecute.

5. Safe systems of work

Employers must also ensure what are known as 'safe systems of work', which means creating an environment that is conducive to health and safety. This can be as basic as making sure that buildings are in good repair, that proper heat and ventilation are provided, and that the workplace is clean and hygienic to work in. However, it may also mean having clear procedures and checklists to make sure that safety is implemented. In some cases, a permit to work may be required in order to carry out certain jobs. A 'safe system of work' should also document what to do in the event of accidents and emergencies.

Make a note of any points from this section that you need to act on.

Notes

_____

_____

_____

_____

_____

_____

_____

ELECTRICITY AT WORK REGULATIONS 1989

The three main hazards associated with electricity are contact with live parts, fire and explosion. Every year about 1000 accidents are reported involving

electrical shock and burns. At least 30 of these are fatal. Many more such incidents go unreported.

Fires started by faulty electrical installations cause many deaths and injuries. Explosions too are caused by electrical apparatus or static electricity igniting flammable vapours or dusts.

It is easy to forget that the ordinary 240-volt, 13 amp domestic plug voltage is strong enough to kill. In business and industry the use of electricity entails far greater risks not only because more sophisticated and powerful equipment is involved, but also because of the environment and conditions in which it is used. - restaurant - a hectic + stressful environment.

Some of the requirements of the Electricity at Work Regulations 1989 are summarized below.

1. Equipment and conditions

Proper equipment and working conditions must be supplied and created. If possible, this means reducing voltage. For instance, lighting can be run at 12 or 25 volts and portable tools must be run at 110 volts from an isolating transformer. Safety devices should be provided, and installation must be carried out professionally and in accordance with full safety regulations.

2. Training

All staff using electrical equipment must receive adequate training and information not only on the safe operation of that equipment but also in respect of the dangers of electricity. For example, would you know what to do if someone received an electric shock?

3. Access and lighting

Adequate access, lighting, fuse boxes and isolators must be made available for all electrical installations.

4. Live working

Live working must not be allowed on any equipment unless absolutely necessary. Before work begins, equipment and power cables must be isolated and the power removed from the installation.

5. Written procedures

Proper safety procedures must be documented and enforced. Anyone carrying out electrical work must be competent to do it safely. This may mean bringing in outside contractors. If this is done, make sure that they belong to a body which checks their work, such as the National Inspection Council for Electrical Installation Contractors.

Other procedures may involve the insulation and armouring of certain power cables, provision of special plugs and replacing frayed and damaged cables quickly and completely. Specific protection equipment – particularly special low voltage equipment in certain situations – and special procedures to deal with overhead electric lines, particularly on building or construction sites, may be necessary.

6. Safety inspections

Inspection of all portable apparatus must be done by a competent person on a regular basis, and this inspection must be documented. Any special requirements such as waterproof or explosion-proof protected equipment must also be assessed.

Make a note on any points from this section that you need to act on.

Notes

_____

_____

_____

_____

_____

COSHH REGULATIONS 1994

COSHH (Control of Substances Hazardous to Health)

The COSHH Regulations were introduced in 1988, updated in 1994 and cover all chemicals, products and materials that may cause damage, injury or discomfort to human beings.

You may also need to consider the Chemicals (Hazard, Information and Packaging) Regulations of 1993. These state that the contents and hazards of any product must be indicated on the package or label.

Safety data sheets should also be provided with any products which you supply.

Many substances can harm you if they enter your body; even many everyday household substances have the potential to cause damage. Special care is needed when handling cancer-causing substances, or flammable, explosive and other more hazardous types of material.

Here are some of the key points as required under the COSHH Regulations.

1. Eliminate and reduce

Wherever possible you should avoid using hazardous substances in your work. The best and most simple way of reducing risk is to eliminate the product or the hazard completely.

2. Give information

The organization and its managers must ensure that proper information exists about the hazards and the products and substances themselves. Every hazardous substance must be labelled and have safety data sheets detailing its storage, transportation and the hazards which it presents.

3. Maintain awareness

People using the products should be aware of the hazards, how they could be affected, what to do to keep themselves and others safe, how to use control equipment and personal protection equipment, how to check and identify when things are wrong, and the results of any exposure monitoring or health surveillance that you may carry out. They should also have full knowledge of any emergency procedures should a leakage or a spillage occur.

4. Create proper working conditions and procedures

Controls must be put in place, and checks carried out to make sure that they are maintained. This will include not only maintaining plant and equipment but also ventilation levels and also ensuring that people are following the rules. If personal protective equipment is used, this must also be tested and replaced if worn or damaged.

5. Provide training

Full and adequate training must be given to all staff who have to use, or come into contact with, any substance that is considered to be hazardous to health. Asking someone to work with hazardous substances without proper training is an offence under the Regulations.

6. Carry out risk assessments

In addition, risk assessments must be carried out regularly. These must consider the hazards of the substances or their ingredients, the route into the body – that is, whether they can be inhaled, swallowed or absorbed through the skin – and the worst potential outcome. You should also know the concentration or conditions likely to cause ill-health and the initial symptoms of overexposure.

A risk assessment must also calculate who could potentially be exposed and who might be accidentally exposed, and estimate how many people might possibly be involved. The assessment must also allow for how often people come into contact with this substance – that is, how often or how intensively or how long they are working with the substances.

Risk assessments must be written down and fully documented. Special assessments are required for lead and asbestos, which have their own separate legislation due to the extreme hazards that each of these now represent. If you use either of these substances, or are likely to come into contact with them, you must be fully aware of the regulations controlling them.

7. Monitor health

Regular checks and health monitoring may also be required, depending on your level of usage and the substances involved. These may require sampling of air, as well as other medical and health checks. These must be carried out regularly and records kept – in some cases, for up to 40 years.

Make a note of any points from this section that concern you.

Notes

_____

_____

_____

_____

_____

_____

_____

MANUAL HANDLING OPERATIONS REGULATIONS 1992

The Manual Handling Operations Regulations were introduced in 1992 as part of an EC directive on Health and Safety. The Workplace (Health, Safety and Welfare) Regulations 1992 also put some emphasis on manual handling operations. The main requirements of these Regulations are as follows.

1. Provide information and training

All employees must be aware of the common hazards that are associated with manually moving loads and frequent forced or awkward movements of the body. They must understand how these can lead, for example, to back injuries and other injuries to the hands, wrists, arms, legs and neck.

2. Maintain safe practice

Employees should be trained on how to lift safely, as well as how to use any lifting or manual handling equipment or facilities provided. These include hoists, trolleys, trucks, steps and so on.

3. Eliminate lifting where possible

It is also important to eliminate manual handling wherever possible. The Regulations state that you must avoid manual handling if a safer method – for example, mechanical lifting – is practicable. This may mean designing jobs to fit the work to the person rather than the person to the work, taking into account human capabilities and limitations and improving efficiency as well as safety. An organization must avoid manual handling, therefore, wherever there is a risk of injury. Any hazardous manual handling operation that cannot be avoided must be properly assessed for risk of injury. Therefore employees should not be asked to lift heavy or awkward objects if:

- ◆ they have not been trained

- ◆ they are above the safe limits and therefore represent an unreasonable level of risk of injury.

4. Provide lifting aids

Wherever possible, equipment and lifting aids should be provided; and this equipment should be tested and safe for the use intended. People must be trained in its usage, and it must be regularly maintained.

5. If you cannot eliminate, reduce where you can

Where manual handling cannot be eliminated, it must be reduced. Actions to consider might include:

- ◆ providing mechanical help such as a sack truck or hoist

- ◆ making loads smaller or lighter or easier to grasp

- ◆ changing the system of work to reduce the effort required

- ◆ improving the layout of the workplace to make the work more efficient

Protective clothing may also be needed to protect parts of the body, such as hands and feet, when lifting.

6. Carry out risk assessments

All manual handling operations must be assessed for risk, and the risk assessment must be properly documented. One particular hazard that may need special attention is that of repetitive handling, since repeated or awkward movements which are either too forceful, too fast or are carried out for too long can lead to disorders of the arms, hands or legs.

Occupations such as typing, working on a till, assembly work and so on are particularly hazardous. The assessment should investigate the gripping, squeezing or pressure required, awkward hand or arm movements, repeated continuous movements, and their speed, as well as the level of intensity and breaks afforded to the worker.

Make a note on any points from this section that you need to act on.

Notes

_____

_____

_____

_____

NOISE AT WORK REGULATIONS 1989

Loud noise at work can cause irreversible hearing damage. It accelerates the normal hearing loss which usually occurs as we grow older. It can also cause other problems such as tinnitus (persistent, troublesome noises in the ear) and affect our ability to communicate effectively, which in turn can cause great personal stress. The Noise at Work Regulations 1989 are intended to reduce hearing damage caused by loud noise and they lay down three levels of action. They require employees to take action when noise reaches the 85-decibel action first level and further action if it reaches the 90-decibel second level or the 140-decibel peak action level. The key requirements of the Regulations are outlined below.

1. Noise monitoring

First, you must determine the actual noise levels in the workplace, using the appropriate sophisticated equipment. If you cannot hear clearly what someone is saying when you are about two metres away the level is likely to be around 85 decibels or higher, and if you cannot hear someone clearly when you are about one metre away the level is likely to be around 90 decibels or higher. If you consider that the noise from a loud radio in a normal room is probably around 70–75 decibels, that traffic noise when standing on the pavement of a busy street is between 80–85 decibels, and that the engine noise when standing very close to a heavy lorry would be in the region of 90–100 decibels, you can see that it does not take much noise to begin to put our hearing at risk.

2. Noise levels

The Regulations require that noise is kept below certain levels, and that the workplace is categorized accordingly. The first level, at which noise does not exceed 85 decibels, is a normal working environment. However, protection must be made freely available to those who want it or request it when the level exceeds 85 decibels. At the second action level, at which noise exceeds 90 decibels, these areas must be properly marked and hearing protection must be compulsory. Nevertheless, it is important to remember that hearing protection is no substitute for noise reduction or eliminating the hazard in the first place.

3. Ear protection

Proper ear protection must be provided for and worn by all employees, and others who either request it or are required to work in a second or third action level zone. You must ensure that the hearing protection is fitted correctly and is worn properly. It should be regularly checked and maintained, and be comfortable and convenient to wear. This equipment should be made available at no cost.

4. Training

All employees working in noisy areas must be fully trained not only on the hazards but also on the wearing of protective hearing equipment. Information and advice must be made freely available and should be clearly displayed.

5. Hearing tests

Hearing tests should be made available to all workers working in high noise areas and should be made available to any workers who believe that their hearing is being affected as a result of noise at work.

6. Reduction of noise

The Regulations put great emphasis on the importance of reducing noise – by eliminating the source of the noise in the first place – rather than protecting workers from that noise. This may mean changing equipment or machinery, organizing the workplace differently, and using acoustic enclosures wherever possible.

Make a note on any points from this section that you need to act on.

Notes

_____

_____

_____

_____

_____

_____

_____

FIRE PRECAUTIONS ACT 1971

Depending on your type of building, you may need a fire certificate. This will depend on the kind of business which you run and the number of people employed in your building. Your local fire authority can offer advice in this area.

You must also have clear and well communicated fire procedures that are tested regularly. This, of course, includes fire drills, but also ensuring that staff know what to do if they discover a fire, or have to telephone for the emergency services.

All reasonable steps must be taken to prevent fire occurring in the first place and to reduce the risk of fire. This may mean reconsidering the type of equipment that you are using, materials and substances that you use, and how these substances are stored. If you are using flammable liquids, can these be reduced or eliminated or their use kept to a restricted area?

All staff must be trained in safety procedures, and information made freely available regarding the use of fire equipment and fire exits.

Regular checks must be made on all fire safety equipment. These should be written down and documented, and must include all extinguishers, fire alarms and other forms of fire emergency equipment. In addition, fire doors and escape routes must be checked, both for operation and to ensure that the regulations are not being breached.

The company should have clear procedures and regulations in respect of precautions needed to safeguard against fire and what to do in the unfortunate event of its occurrence. The Act requires both employers and employees to take every practical measure in making sure that these regulations are fully implemented.

Make a note on any points from this section that you need to act on.

Notes

_____

_____

_____

_____

_____

_____

_____

DISPLAY SCREEN EQUIPMENT REGULATIONS 1992

These Regulations have been introduced to meet the needs of the changing nature of our workplaces and offices. Over the last ten years the use of computers and visual display units has greatly increased. Workers using VDUs need well designed work areas with suitable lighting and comfortable adjustable seating. This helps reduce eye strain and back or upper limb problems. No special precautions are necessary against radiation.

The requirements of the Regulations cover the following areas.

1. Assessment

All work stations must be assessed regularly, and a record of the assessment must be kept. This is best done at least once every 12 months – more frequently if the workload or equipment is changed.

2. Improvements

Any changes or improvements to equipment or working practices noted in the written assessment must be fully implemented under the guidelines within the Regulations.

3. VDU safety training

All staff who are classified as habitual users of VDU or display screen equipment must be trained in safe working practices. They should also be made aware of the health and safety aspects of their work.

4. Health monitoring

Organizations should also monitor the health of people using VDU equipment. There are obligations to provide eye tests for users on request, and at regular intervals afterwards, and, in certain cases, special spectacles where required.

5. Workloads

Workloads must be organized and planned to allow breaks or changes of activity. This is to avoid undue stress, which may be manifested in the form of headaches, backaches or general fatigue.

6. Work station and environment

In addition, all work stations – that is, the computer or VDU equipment, together with associated peripherals such as printers, desks, chairs and so on – must be assessed to check whether they meet the required standards. Unless the equipment has been manufactured and supplied since the Regulations came into force, it is unlikely to comply with these standards.

Review this section and make some notes on the points that are most applicable or important to you with respect to working within the Regulations.

- ⌨ Regular assessment

- ⌨ Improvements under the guidelines

- ⌨ Training in safe working practices

- ⌨ Health monitoring

- ⌨ Provision of eye tests

- ⌨ Avoidance of undue stress

Notes

_____

_____

_____

_____

_____

_____

_____

WORKPLACE (HEALTH, SAFETY AND WELFARE) REGULATIONS 1992

There can be many dangers at work. Safety hazards include slips, trips and falls, as well as more obvious things such as fire, electricity and hazardous chemicals. Health hazards may also include poor seating, lighting, building repair and ventilation. The Regulations, which apply in full to **all** workplaces, require the assessment of working environments and provide a set of guidelines on how to do this.

The main requirements of these Regulations are as follows.

1. Lighting

The organization must provide good light without glare. This means natural light wherever possible. A good level of local lighting is required in areas where detailed work is carried out. Lighting must be of a suitable form. Some fluorescent tubes flicker and can be dangerous with some types of rotating machinery. Special fittings are required in areas where the atmosphere and/or equipment is flammable or explosive.

2. Heating and ventilation

A reasonable working temperature must be maintained – usually at least 16 °C or 13 °C where strenuous work is performed. In areas where a comfortable temperature cannot be maintained – for instance, in large warehouses – local heating or cooling should be provided. Good ventilation must be provided, especially in areas where fumes or dust may exist, and draughts should be avoided. Heating systems should also be checked to make sure that they do not give off dangerous or offensive levels of fumes.

3. Hygiene

The Regulations specify that there should be sufficient toilets, changing and washing facilities. These include separate toilets for men and women unless each convenience has its own lockable door, wash basins with hot and cold or warm running water, showers for dirty work or emergencies, soap and towels or a hand-dryer, and skin cleansers with nail brushes where necessary. In certain situations – for example, in the serving and preparation of food – special hygiene precautions are required.

A clean drinking water supply should also be made available, together with rest facilities. The organization must also provide facilities to protect non-smokers from discomfort caused by tobacco smoke in any separate rest area – that is, it should provide separate areas or rooms for smokers and non-smokers or prohibit smoking in rest areas and rest rooms.

4. General safety

People should be able to move around the premises safely. This means safe routes for pedestrians and vehicles and level, even surfaces without broken boards, obstructions or holes. Surfaces should also be maintained so that they do not become slippery. Passageways and stairways must be well lit and kept clear of obstacles and obstructions. Hand-rails should be fitted on all stairways and ramps used where necessary. Vision panels should be installed in swing-doors.

5. Equipment

The Regulations also require that safety equipment is provided and maintained and that the provision for this is appropriate to the place of work.

Make a note on any points from this section that you need to act on.

Notes

_____

_____

_____

_____

_____

_____

_____

_____

MANAGEMENT OF HEALTH AND SAFETY AT WORK REGULATIONS 1992

The Management of Health and Safety at Work Regulations make specific demands on managers and directors, as well as on health and safety officers, with regard to their responsibilities in assessing and managing risk. In simple terms, this means identifying hazards and quantifying and reducing risk.

- ◆ A hazard is anything that has the potential to cause harm (for example, chemicals, electricity, working from ladders and so on)

- ◆ A risk is the likelihood (great or small) of harm actually being done.

For example, consider a can of solvent on a shelf. There is a hazard if the solvent is toxic or flammable, but very little risk. The risk increases when it is taken down from the shelf and poured into a bucket. Harmful vapour is given off and there is a danger of spillage. The situation is made much worse if a mop is then used to spread it over the floor for cleaning. The chance of harm – that is, the risk – is then high. This type of analysis is known as risk assessment.

The principal requirements of the Regulations are set out below.

1. Competence

Any risk assessment must be carried out by a 'competent person' – in other words, someone who has the necessary technical expertise, training and experience to carry out the examination or test. This could be an outside organization, such as an insurance company or individual, or one of your own staff. They should know not only the health and safety aspects, but also have a good understanding of the job and the task involved.

2. Regularity

Assessments should be made regularly and be in the form of a written document.

3. Implementation

Assessments must be acted on. Carrying out a risk assessment which identifies hazards and risks is not sufficient.

4. Training

All members of staff should receive proper health and safety training, at regular intervals. This training should be appropriate to both their level of experience and the tasks required of them.

Make a note on any points from this section that you need to act on.

Notes

_____

_____

_____

_____

_____

_____

Chapter 3
Understanding
Safety in the
Workplace

Now that you are aware of the regulations, here is how they are applied in the workplace.

Before starting this chapter, please take a few moments to make a note of any ideas or actions in the learning diary and log in Chapter 1.

THERE IS NO SUCH THING AS AN ACCIDENT

Workplace accidents are caused by people. More accurately, they are caused by what they do or don't do.

Equipment and machinery may sometimes break down, and incidents may occur which cause accidents, but they are nearly always traceable to some degree of human error, negligence or ignorance.

Workplace accidents happen to ordinary people. Although we may like to think that accidents only happen to other people, or believe that we are somehow cleverer, better, luckier or more organized than other people, in reality, an accident can happen to any one of us at any time. It could happen to you or me; it could happen today or tomorrow, next month or next year.

How aware are you of safety in your day-to-day work?

Study assignment:

Look around your normal workplace, and the room in which you are working now and identify as many potential hazards as you can.

Find at least five.

1.

2.

3.

4.

5.

The dictionary defines an accident as 'an unforeseen event' or 'a misfortune or mishap, especially causing injury or death'. However, the safety statistics tell us that we can predict accidents because we know what the causes are and, if we see the causes occurring, we can be sure that there is an accident waiting to happen somewhere along the line.

ACCIDENT STATISTICS

How many people do you think suffer disabling injuries every year whilst at work?

a) 10 000 or less   b) 100 000   c) 1 000 000 or more

How many people do you think are killed at work every year?

a) 10 or less   b) 100   c) 500 or more

How many working days do you think are lost every year in the UK because of accidents, sickness or injury?

a) 1 million   b) 5 million   c) 10 million or more

What do you think are the three most common accidents at work?

1.

2.

3.

**PLEASE COMPLETE
BEFORE CONTINUING**

ACCIDENT STATISTICS

For an industrialized nation like ours, with a reasonably good record of health and safety awareness, the statistics are quite surprising. Every year over 30 million working days are lost because of work-related accidents, sickness or injury.

A casual attitude can often result in a casualty!

There are hundreds of thousands of workplace accidents every year and, at any one time, several million people are suffering ill-health, either caused or made worse by work conditions. Furthermore, on average, every working day there are at least two fatal injuries in the workplace. This means that, tonight, somebody, somewhere, will not be going home.

Workplace accidents are more common than you might think.

Accidents can happen to any of us at any time. They are not a rarity. Fortunately, they are also not that common, but we do need to make sure that we do not become another statistic.

Here are some more painful statistics illustrating the most common types of accident and their associated causes. These figures were produced by the Health and Safety Commission's *Annual Statistics Report* and refer to the most commonly occurring accidents, that have been reported. (There are, of course, many more – possibly a much larger number – that go unreported.)

For employees:

1.	Slips, trips or falls (on the same level)	25%
2.	Falls from height	21%
3.	Injuries from moving, falling or flying objects	12%

For the self-employed:

1.	Falls from height	45%
2.	Slips, trips or falls (on the same level)	15%
3.	Injuries from a moving, falling or flying object	14%

These statistics are for the most recent period available. However, the HSC comments that 'Whilst most other accidents stayed relatively unchanged, slip, trip or fall accidents have increased from 26% to 35% for employees for the period 1986 to 1996'. These figures do not take into account illness or sickness that may be caused by repetitive strain or cumulative injuries.

So, in summary, there are 1.6 million accidents at work each year; 2.2 million people are currently suffering ill-health caused, or made worse, by work conditions; 30 million working days per year are lost; and every year about 500 people are killed at work and several thousand more are permanently disabled through work-related accidents or injuries.

The most common workplace accidents

◆ **Straining the body**
  – twisting, reaching or stretching

◆ **Moving or falling objects**
  – most common damage to head, fingers, feet and eyes

◆ **Slips, trips and falls**
  – from minor grazes to a broken neck

◆ **Getting caught in a machine**
  – belts, pulleys, slicers, grinders, and so on

◆ **Injuries caused by hazardous chemicals**
  – inhalation or direct exposure

◆ **Hearing loss or damage**
  – loud noise can destroy or damage hearing

◆ **Electric shock**
  – almost **any** electric tool or appliance can kill

◆ **Eye damage**
  – flying objects, splashing liquids, intense heat or light

A moment's carelessness – a lifetime's regret.

Please make a note of any points from this section that concern you.

Notes

_____

_____

_____

_____

_____

_____

_____

WORKPLACE SAFETY AWARENESS

Many people, when first discussing the topic of workplace safety, ask the question, 'But our workplaces are safe aren't they?'. The answer, of course, is that they can be, but only if we make safety a priority. Your workplace is as safe, or as dangerous and hazardous, as you choose to make it. However, workplace 'accidents' may not be accidents at all.

Many workplace accidents are cumulative and take years to take effect. For instance, RSI, or repetitive strain injury, can be the result of years of neglect or poor practice in doing repetitive tasks – often very small repetitive movements, as in using a keyboard or operating machinery in an intense or prolonged fashion. The effects of these injuries are sometimes very far-reaching.

Good housekeeping

Much of good safety is really just good common sense, and as we walk around our workplaces on a daily basis we must keep in mind what could generally be summarized as good housekeeping. In 1992 a new series of Regulations, Workplace (Health, Safety and Welfare) Regulations 1992, were introduced to update the ageing Offices, Shops and Railway Premises Act 1963 and the Factories Act 1961. These new Regulations take account of new working conditions, new working styles and new technology in the work environment. However, the basic fundamental principles remain the same – think safety; act safety; be safe.

Here are seven keys to good safety awareness.

1. Walk areas

Walk areas must be kept clear and tidy. This does not just apply to emergency exits, fire exits or areas through which customers may be walking. **All** walk areas must be kept clear and free of debris, rubbish, boxes and other obstructions.

2. Drawers

Leaving drawers open can cause a very annoying and pointless accident – particularly as they are so simple to close!

3. Chemicals

Chemicals must be stored and labelled correctly, whether this is correcting fluid, floor cleaners, polishes, abrasives or specialized chemicals used in our work. Failure to do so is a breach of the law.

Being safe simply means knowing what to do (and what NOT to do), and then DOING what you know.

4. Ventilation and heating

The organization must provide a reasonable working temperature in all workrooms, local heating or cooling systems where a comfortable temperature cannot be maintained and good ventilation. Draughts and heating systems giving off dangerous or offensive levels of fumes must be avoided. In addition, workrooms should be spacious enough to work comfortably in, and arrangements should be made to protect non-smokers from discomfort caused by tobacco smoke.

5. Safety signs

These must be provided at all appropriate points and for all valid reasons. They must be in good condition and clearly displayed. People should also be aware of their meaning, either through explanation or training. Whilst many are very self-explanatory, others are slightly more complicated and you may need to understand what these mean.

> **Safety signs:**
>
> *A safety sign with a blue background and white writing signifies a mandatory – must do – instruction.*
>
> *A safety sign with a yellow background and black writing signifies a warning – care and caution – instruction.*
>
> *A safety sign with a red background and white writing signifies a fire equipment instruction.*
>
> *A safety sign with a green background and white writing signifies safe conditions – for example, fire escapes, exits, first aid box and so on.*
>
> *A safety sign with a diamond shape and either a red, blue, yellow, white or green background and black writing signifies that a package or load contains hazardous substances.*

6. First aid

Every workplace environment should have first aid equipment, a trained first-aider and detailed procedures to follow in the event of personal accident or injury. There should also be an accident book and a record kept of all uses of first aid equipment.

7. *Noise*

This must be controlled. Noise should either be eliminated or kept to an absolute minimum and, where noisy environments cannot be avoided, protective equipment must be issued and worn.

8. *Hygiene*

Clean and well ventilated toilets with wash basins, hot and cold running water and drinking water must be provided.

Make a note of any points from this section that concern you.

Notes

_____

_____

_____

_____

_____

_____

_____

IDENTIFYING HAZARDS AND RISKS

Understanding hazards and risks

♦ A hazard is anything that has the potential to cause harm (for example, chemicals, electricity, working from ladders and so on).

♦ A risk is the likelihood (great or small) of harm being done.

As an example, consider a can of solvent on a shelf. There is a hazard if the solvent is toxic or flammable, but very little risk. The risk increases when it is taken down and poured into a bucket. Harmful vapour is given off and there is a danger of spillage. The situation is made much worse if a mop is then used to spread it over the floor for cleaning. The chance of harm – that is, the risk – is then high.

You will see the term 'risk assessment' used in regulations and guidance. Do not be put off by this phrase – it concerns doing things described in this chapter.

Who might be at risk?

♦ workers – including those off-site

♦ visitors to your premises – for example, cleaners, contractors

♦ the public – for example, when calling in to buy your products.

Look for the hazards – walk around your workplace. Imagine what might go wrong at each stage of each task being carried out. Here are some typical activities which carry a risk of accidents:

♦ receipt of raw materials – for example, when lifting or carrying

♦ stacking and storage – for example, falling objects and materials, exposure to toxic substances

♦ movement of people and materials – for example, falls, collisions, processing of raw materials, exposure to chemicals, maintenance of buildings, such as roof work and gutter cleaning

♦ maintenance of plant and machinery – for example, lifting tackle, equipment using electricity

♦ distribution of finished goods – for example, movement of vehicles dealing with emergencies, spillages, fires.

In many businesses most accidents are caused by a few key activities. Ignore the trivial and concentrate on those that could cause serious harm. But don't just look at the obvious ones – operations such as roof work, maintenance and transport movements (including fork-lift trucks) cause far more deaths and serious injuries each year than many mainstream activities.

Assess the risk

First, consider any accidents which you may have suffered. What happened? What was the hazard? How high was the risk? What was its nature? How could it have been minimized?

Then, consider the tasks being carried out in your own workplace:

◆ What is the worst result of an accident? Is it a broken finger, someone suffering permanent lung damage or death?

◆ How likely is it to happen? How often is the job done? How close do people get to the hazard? How likely is it that something can go wrong?

◆ How many people could be hurt if things did go wrong? Could this include people who don't work for you?

Don't forget non-production tasks, off-site activities and work done outside normal working hours. You should know what your main risks are.

Are the main risks under control?

You now need to see if you are taking the right precautions. You may already be doing enough, but how can you be certain?

Look at the work, talk to people and check records. Find out what really goes on, and not what you think goes on.

Make improvements

If you find that more needs to be done, ask yourself if you can eliminate the hazard by doing the job in a different way – for example, by using a different, safer chemical or buying materials already cut to size instead of doing it yourself. If you cannot, you should consider controlling the hazard in some other way.

◆ Deal with the hazards that carry most risk first.

◆ Set realistic dates for each of the improvements needed.

◆ Don't try to do everything at once.

- ◆ Remember to agree precautions with the workforce, working together to solve problems.

- ◆ Don't forget that new training and information could be needed.

- ◆ Check that precautions remain in place.

If you find that you have quite a lot to do, consider preparing an action plan, stating what you will do and when.

Remember that situations and circumstances change – new materials come in, machines wear out and break down and need regular maintenance, rules are broken and people don't always do as they've been told.

The only way to find out about such changes as these is to check. Don't wait until something goes wrong, but, equally, don't try to check everything at once. Deal with a few key issues at a time, starting with the main hazards which you identified earlier. Doing this also lets people know that checks will be made and that you are interested in what is happening day-to-day in the workplace – not just when things have gone wrong.

Don't forget maintenance

Be guided by manufacturers' recommendations when working out your own maintenance schedules for such items as vehicles, fork-lift trucks, ventilation plant, ladders, portable electrical equipment, protective clothing and equipment and machine guards.

Remember, checks are no substitute for maintenance.

Safety inspectors and the law

Health and Safety laws that apply to your business are enforced by inspectors either from the Health and Safety Executive (HSE) or from your local council. Their job is to see how well you are dealing with your workplace hazards, especially the more serious ones which could lead to injuries or ill-health. They may wish to investigate an accident or a complaint.

Inspectors do visit workplaces without notice but you are entitled to see their identification before admitting them.

Don't forget that they are there to give help and advice, particularly to smaller firms which may not be well informed. When they do find problems they will aim to deal with you in a reasonable and fair way. If you are not satisfied with the way in which you have been treated, take the matter up with the inspector's manager, whose name will be given on all letters from the HSE. Your complaint will certainly be investigated, and you will be told what must be done to correct the situation if a fault is found.

Inspectors do have wide powers that include the right of entry to your premises, the right to talk to employees and safety representatives and the right to take photographs and samples. They are entitled to your cooperation and answers to questions.

If there is a problem, they have the right to issue a notice requiring improvements to be made, or (where a risk of a serious personal injury exists) one that stops a process or the use of dangerous equipment. If you receive an improvement or prohibition notice you have the right to appeal to an industrial tribunal.

Inspectors do have the power to prosecute a business or, under certain circumstances, an individual for breaking Health and Safety law, but they will take your attitude and safety record into account.

How often do you need to check?

Some important items may have to be checked daily, while others can safely be left for much longer. This is a matter for you to decide, except in cases where the law requires some inspections or examinations to be carried out by specially appointed people.

Here are some key examples:

- ◆ Ventilation systems must be examined and tested every 14 months.

- ◆ Power press guards must be inspected at each shift.

- ◆ Scaffolds must be inspected weekly.

- ◆ Rescue equipment must be examined monthly.

- ◆ Other periodic tests and examinations must be carried out by a **'competent person'**.

Who is a competent person?

Someone who has the necessary technical expertise, training and experience to carry out the examination or test. This could be an outside organization such as an insurance company or other inspecting organization, a self-employed person or one of your own staff who is capable of doing the task. For example, an electrician, trained to the formal and required procedures, should carry out tests on electrical equipment and installations.

Make a note of any points from this section that concern you.

Notes

_____

_____

_____

_____

_____

_____

_____

HAZARDS AND RISKS

When answering the questions below, consider not only your experience in this job, but in previous ones.

What hazards and risks exist in your workplace? (Please give examples and be specific.)

How can you begin to assess which are more significant than others?

Hazards	Risks

**PLEASE COMPLETE
BEFORE CONTINUING**

Chapter 4
Practical Risk Assessment

This chapter guides you through the process of making a risk assessment.

Before starting this chapter, please take a few moments to make a note of any ideas or actions in the learning diary and log in Chapter 1.

HOW TO ASSESS RISKS IN THE WORKPLACE

What is a risk assessment?

An assessment of risk is nothing more than a careful examination of what, in your work, could cause harm to people, so that you can weigh up whether you have taken enough precautions or should do more to prevent harm.

The aim is to make sure that no one gets hurt or becomes ill. Accidents and ill-health can ruin lives and also affect your business too if output is lost, machinery damaged, insurance costs increase or you have to go to court.

> *A hazard is anything that has the potential to cause harm (for example, chemicals, electricity, working from ladders and so on).*
>
> *A risk is the likelihood (great or small) of harm being done.*

The important things which you need to decide are whether a hazard is significant, and whether you have taken satisfactory precautions to minimize the associated risk. You should check this aspect when you assess the risks. For instance, electricity can kill but the risk of it doing so in an office environment is remote, provided that 'live' components are insulated and metal casings are properly earthed.

How do you make a risk assessment?

First, it is important not to overcomplicate the task. In most firms in the commercial, service and light industrial sector, the hazards are few and simple. Checking them is a matter of common sense, but nevertheless necessary. You may have already assessed some of them – for example, if you use toxic or dangerous chemicals, you should already have made an assessment of the risks to health and the precautions which you need to take under the Control of Substances Hazardous to Health Regulations (COSHH).

If so, you can consider them 'checked', and write that down if you are making a written assessment. For other hazards, you probably already know whether you have machinery that could cause harm, or if there is an awkward entrance or stairway which might cause an accident. If so, check that you have taken what reasonable precautions you can to avoid injury.

If you are a small firm and you are confident that you understand the work, you can carry out the assessment yourself.

If you belong to a larger firm, you could ask a responsible employee, safety representative or safety officer to help you. If you are not confident, get help from a competent source. Remember, you are responsible for making sure that the assessment is carried out to an adequate standard.

Make a note on any points from this section that concern you.

Notes

_____

_____

_____

_____

_____

_____

_____

_____

_____

_____

_____

STEP 1: LOOK FOR THE HAZARDS

If you are doing the assessment yourself, walk around your workplace and look afresh at what could reasonably be expected to cause harm. Ignore the trivial and concentrate only on significant hazards that could result in serious harm or affect several people.

Ask your employees or their representatives what they think. They may have noticed potential problems that are not immediately obvious.

Manufacturers' instructions or data sheets can also help you identify the hazards and put risks in their true perspective, as can accident and ill-health records.

Make a note on any points from this section that you need to act on.

Notes

_____

_____

_____

_____

_____

_____

_____

_____

RISK ASSESSMENT: PART 1

Make a list of some of the jobs, tasks and operations that you or other people perform.

For each one identify as many hazards as you can.

Job, task, operation	Hazards

**PLEASE COMPLETE
BEFORE CONTINUING**

STEP 2: DECIDE WHO MIGHT BE HARMED, AND HOW

You have a responsibility under the law to safeguard anybody who might be affected by what you do.

Consider people who may not be in the workplace all the time – for example, cleaners, visitors, contractors, maintenance personnel and so on.

Include members of the public, or people with whom you share your workplace, if there is a chance that they could be harmed by your activities.

Make a note on any points from this section that you need to act on.

Notes

_____

_____

_____

_____

_____

_____

_____

_____

STEP 3: EVALUATE THE RISKS

Evaluate the risks arising from the hazards and decide whether existing precautions are adequate or whether more should be done.

Even after all precautions have been taken, a degree of risk usually remains. What you have to decide, for each significant hazard, is whether this remaining risk is high, medium or low. First, ask yourself whether you have done everything that the law requires. For example, there are legal requirements that restrict access to dangerous parts of machinery.

Then ask yourself whether generally accepted industry standards are in place. But don't stop there, because the law also says that you must do what is reasonably practicable to keep your workplace safe. Your real aim is to minimize all risks by adding to your precautions if necessary.

Make a note on any points from this section that you need to act on.

Notes

_____

_____

_____

_____

_____

_____

_____

RISK ASSESSMENT: PART 2 – RISK EVALUATION

Now list all the hazards that you wrote down previously and rate each one on a scale of 1–5 for the degree of harm that may be caused, and A to E for the chance of that harm happening – that is, the risk.

Hazards: on a scale of 1–5

Score 5 as the highest and 1 as the lowest. For instance, a number 5 hazard with the potential to cause very serious harm – for example, a cleaning process which produces toxic fumes. Also increase the hazard rating if a number of people may be involved or affected.

Risks: A to E for the likelihood of harm being caused

Score A as the highest and E as the lowest. An 'A' category risk would be one with a very high (80 per cent or more) chance of happening and E with a very remote (10 per cent or less) chance of happening. An example might be using an electric drill. Whilst it can kill, the chances (or 'risk') of that happening in an office where everything is properly installed and earthed is small.

Hazard	Hazard scale (1–5)	Risk rating (A–E)

> **PLEASE COMPLETE**
> **BEFORE CONTINUING**

STEP 4: RECORD YOUR FINDINGS

If you have fewer than five employees you need not write anything down, but if you have five or more employees you must record the significant findings of your assessment in writing.

This means:

1. writing down the more significant hazards

and

2. recording your most important conclusions – for example, 'Electrical installations: insulation and earth checked and found sound' or 'Fumes from welding: local exhaust ventilation provided and regularly checked'.

You must also inform your employees about your findings. There is no need to show how you did your assessment, provided that you can show that:

♦ a proper check was made

♦ you asked who might be affected

♦ you dealt with all the obvious significant hazards, taking into account the number of people who could be involved.

Assessments need to be suitable and sufficient, not perfect. The critical questions are:

♦ Are the precautions reasonable?

♦ Is there something to show that a proper check was made?

Keep written documents for future reference or use; it can help if an inspector later questions your precautions, or if you become involved in any action for civil liability. Such documents can also remind you to keep an eye on particular matters, and help show that you have done what the law requires.

To make things simpler, you can refer to other documents, such as manuals, the arrangements in your health and safety policy statement, company rules, manufacturers' instructions, and your health and safety procedures. These may already list hazards and precautions. You don't need to repeat all that, and it is up to you whether you combine all the documents or keep them separately.

Make a note on any points from this section that you need to act on.

Notes

STEP 5: NEW SAFETY MEASURES

Improving health and safety need not cost much. Placing a mirror on a dangerous blind corner to help prevent vehicle accidents and covering slippery steps with non-slip material are inexpensive precautions considering the risks which these hazards entail. Also consider training, more safety notices and changing working practices. If you find that you need to take action to improve health and safety, ask yourself:

- **Can I eliminate the hazard altogether?**

- **If not, how can I control the risks so that harm is unlikely?**

Only resort to personal protective equipment when there is nothing else that you can reasonably do.

If the work you do tends to vary greatly, or if you or your employees move from one site to another, select those hazards that you can reasonably foresee and assess the risks from them. After that, if you notice any unusual hazard when you arrive on a site, obtain information from others on-site, and take what action seems necessary.

If you share a workplace, tell the other employers and self-employed people there about any risks which your work could cause them, and what precautions you are taking. In addition, think about the risks to your workforce from those who share your workplace.

Make a note on any points from this section that you need to act on.

Notes

_____

_____

_____

_____

_____

RISK ASSESSMENT: PART 3

Using the assessment of hazards which you made in the previous exercise, select the most significant. Review each one in turn and consider the following questions.

Can the hazard be removed or prevented altogether?

What else can be done to reduce and control the risks associated with this hazard?

Hazard	Steps to remove or reduce risk

PLEASE COMPLETE
BEFORE CONTINUING

REVIEW YOUR ASSESSMENT REGULARLY

Review your assessment from time to time and revise it if necessary.

Eventually you will introduce new machines, substances and procedures that could lead to new hazards. If there is any significant change, you should add to the assessment to take account of the new hazard. In any case, it is good practice to review your assessment periodically. Don't amend your assessment for every trivial change or for each new job, but if a new job introduces significant new hazards of its own, you will want to consider them in their own right and do whatever you need to keep the risks down.

Make a note on any points from this section that you need to act on.

Notes

RISK ASSESSMENT FORM CHECKLIST

Select one safety area and create a sample risk assessment form or checklist. You might find it helpful to group your points or questions under the following headings which must all be covered, ideally in some detail.

- Company name, address/location

- Date of assessment and assessor, next review date

- What hazards exist?

- Who might be at risk?

- What safety measures are in place?

- What further action needs to be taken?

PLEASE COMPLETE
BEFORE CONTINUING

PLANNING A RISK ASSESSMENT

What do you consider to be the most important things you should or shouldn't do when carrying out a risk assessment?

Dos	Don'ts

**PLEASE COMPLETE
BEFORE CONTINUING**

Chapter 5
Learning Review

This chapter tests your knowledge and understanding of risk assessment and safety awareness.

Before starting this chapter, please take a few moments to make a note of any ideas or actions in the learning diary and log in Chapter 1.

TEST YOUR KNOWLEDGE (1)

1.   Give a definition of 'risk assessment'.

2.   What is the purpose of carrying out risk assessments?

3.   Define the terms 'hazard' and 'risk'.

4.   Who (groups of people) do you need to consider when performing a risk assessment?

5.   List three sets of legislation of which you may need to be aware.

   1.

   2.

   3.

6.   Is it a legal requirement to complete a risk assessment for all employees or only those working with significant hazards or higher risk areas?

7.   When making recommendations is cost an excuse for not implementing certain measures?

> **PLEASE COMPLETE**
> **BEFORE CONTINUING**

TEST YOUR KNOWLEDGE (2)

1. List three benefits to the organization of carrying out proper risk
    assessments.

    1.

    2.

    3.

2. List three benefits to employees of carrying out proper risk assessments.

    1.

    2.

    3.

3. Give an example of a significant hazard from your own work
    environment and the level of risk associated with this.

4. For the hazard identified above, detail some of the ways in which the
    risk could be reduced.

5. How often should you complete a risk assessment?

6. What are the penalties for the companies and individuals that fail in
    their duty to carry out suitable risk assessments?

7. What are the requirements for someone being authorized or able to
    carry out a risk assessment?

8. Apart from the passage of time, what factors or circumstances might
    cause a new risk assessment to be required?

> **PLEASE COMPLETE**
> **BEFORE CONTINUING**

TEST YOUR KNOWLEDGE (3)

1. What does HASAWA stand for?

2. Small firms (employing less than 50 employees) have a worse record of safety than larger firms.

   TRUE/FALSE

3. Why do you think this is?

4. How many accidents occur at work every year?

   a) 600 000

   b) 1 600 000

   c) 2 200 000

5. How many people, at any one time, are suffering ill-health, either caused, or made worse, by work conditions?

   a) 600 000

   b) 1 600 000

   c) 2 200 000

6. How many working days are lost each year due to health and safety-related accidents, sickness or injury?

   a) 200

   b) 600

   c) 400

7. What is the most common form of accident/injury?

8. How many people are killed at work every year?

   a) 200

   b) 400

   c) 500

> **PLEASE COMPLETE**
> **BEFORE CONTINUING**

Chapter 6
Risk Assessment Checklists

This chapter contains a collection of example checklists. They can be used as set out or further adapted to meet your workplace risk assessment requirements.

WORKPLACE ASSESSMENT QUESTIONNAIRE

Respond to these questions, keeping your place of work in mind, and complete as accurately and fully as possible.

	Y/N	Notes
1. Are workers free from draughts or excessive air movement?		
2. If the workplace sometimes gets too warm, have steps been taken to reduce the temperature?		
3. Are thermometers available to allow staff to check temperatures?		
4. Is the temperature in the workplace level (min. 16 °C)?		
5. If extremes of cold cannot be avoided, are staff provided with suitable protective clothing?		
6. Are the floor coverings adequate?		
7. If portable heating appliances are used, are they safe to use in the workplace and carefully placed?		
8. Are heating and ventilation facilities regularly inspected and serviced?		
9. Is there sufficient fresh air in the workplace and is it free from fumes and odours?		

What, in your opinion, are the three most important points to consider for this assessment?

> 1.
>
> 2.
>
> 3.

DISPLAY SCREEN EQUIPMENT QUESTIONNAIRE

Respond to these questions, keeping your place of work in mind, and complete as accurately and fully as possible.

	Y/N	Notes
1. Is the work desk large enough to allow flexibility and comfort?		
2. Is the chair stable and of the right type?		
3. Does it allow the operator freedom of movement?		
4. Is the height of the chair adjustable?		
5. Is the screen image stable?		
6. When adjusted, is the screen image acceptable?		
7. Is there space in front of the keyboard to support the operator's hands?		
8. Are the symbols on the keys legible?		
9. Is there a document holder available, if required?		
10 Is there enough space for comfort?		
11. Is the working area free from glare?		
12. Does the operator suffer any aches and pains at all?		
13. Are sufficient breaks away from the keyboard allowed for?		

What, in your opinion, are the three most important points to consider for this assessment?

1.

2.

3.

RISK ASSESSMENT QUESTIONNAIRE

Respond to these questions, keeping your place of work in mind, and complete as accurately and fully as possible.

	Y/N	Notes
1. Are staff given suitable and sufficient training, instruction and information on the use of all equipment and the task for which it is used?		
2. Have all electrical installations been tested in accordance with the current Regulations?		
3. Is a permit-to-work system in operation to prevent those doing work being put at risk by others?		
4. Are the doors of electrical switchrooms fitted with 'DANGER 240/415 volts' notices?		
5. Has the recommended testing period been entered on to the Test Certificate?		
6. Is there a notice regarding electrical shocks displayed by the switchgear?		
7. Are all appliance test records available?		
8. In situations where people might fall or trip, or where risks are apparent, is secure fencing provided and are notices visible?		

What, in your opinion, are the three most important points to consider for this assessment?

1.

2.

3.

SAFETY FOR MANAGERS QUESTIONNAIRE

Respond to these questions, keeping your place of work in mind, and complete as accurately and fully as possible.

	Y/N	Notes
1. Do you consult and involve your staff and the safety representatives regularly in health and safety issues?		
2. Does your safety policy clearly specify people's responsibility?		
3. Have you listed some of the responsibilities that you allocate to people for health and safety issues (for example, first-aiders, fire wardens and so on)?		
4. Do your staff have enough information about the risks in their work and how to take preventive steps?		
5. At what stage do you consider health and safety issues when new work routines, equipment or procedures are introduced?		
6. Are all noise precautions regularly checked and records kept?		
7. Have noise checks been performed?		
8. Do you know how many accidents or near-misses occur at work in your department/company every year?		
9. Do you pay attention to changes in legislation?		

What, in your opinion, are the three most important points to consider for this assessment?

1.
2.
3.

FIRE SAFETY QUESTIONNAIRE

Respond to these questions, keeping your place of work in mind, and complete as accurately and fully as possible.

	Y/N	Notes
1. Are sufficient and adequate fire-fighting appliances available?		
2. Are portable fire-fighting appliances of the correct type?		
3. If an automatic fire alarm system exists, is it regularly tested and maintained?		
4. Are fire alarm test and maintenance records kept? Are they up-to-date?		
5. Are all fire-fighting installations and appliances regularly tested and maintained?		
6. Are flammable liquids, chemicals, gases, alcohol and so on stored in accordance with the Regulations?		
7. Are all electrical and mechanical plant rooms free of all unnecessary stored material?		
8. Is there an automatic smoke detection system on all escape routes?		
9. Are all necessary fire signs displayed in appropriate places?		

What, in your opinion, are the three most important points to consider for this assessment?

> 1.
>
> 2.
>
> 3.

Note: Fire Safety is a specialized subject and the professional advice of the Fire Prevention Officer of the local fire authority should be obtained in all circumstances.

OFFICE SAFETY QUESTIONNAIRE

Respond to these questions, keeping your place of work in mind, and complete as accurately and fully as possible.

	Y/N	Notes
1. Are all operations or equipment noise levels below the noise threshold?		
2. Have reasonable and adequate steps been taken to reduce or eliminate noisy operations?		
3. Are all relevant safety signs and notices clearly read and understood?		
4. Are suitable sanitary conveniences provided at readily accessible places?		
5. Are sufficient and adequate sanitary conveniences provided for both men and women and are the rooms properly ventilated and illuminated?		
6. Are sufficient washing facilities available in the vicinity of all sanitary conveniences and changing rooms?		
7. Is the office temperature acceptable most of the time?		
8. Where applicable, are there special sanitary facilities for the disabled?		
9. Is the air quality acceptable?		
10. Is light properly provided and glare controlled?		
11. Are cables tidy and away from walk areas?		

What, in your opinion, are the three most important points to consider for this assessment?

| 1. |
| 2. |
| 3. |

ENVIRONMENTAL AWARENESS QUESTIONNAIRE

Respond to these questions, keeping your place of work in mind, and complete as accurately and fully as possible.

	Y/N	Notes
1. Is the temperature in the workplace controlled at a reasonable level (min. 16 °C)?		
2. If extremes of temperature cannot be avoided, are workers provided with suitable protective outfits?		
3. Are thermometers available at convenient positions to enable staff to check temperatures?		
4. Are products of combustion discharged safely, away from the workplace?		
5. Is sufficient fresh air introduced into the workplace by either natural or mechanical means?		
6. Is the fresh air that is introduced free from impurities, fumes or odours?		
7. Are workers free from draughts or excessive air movement?		

What, in your opinion, are the three most important points to consider for this assessment?

1.

2.

3.

MANUAL HANDLING QUESTIONNAIRE

Respond to these questions, keeping your place of work in mind, and complete as accurately and fully as possible.

	Y/N	Notes
1. Have staff been trained on manual handling techniques and methods?		
2. Is it practical to mechanize or automate any tasks at reasonable cost?		
3. Can moving heavy loads reasonably be avoided?		
4. Is there stated permission for rest and/or recovery periods?		
5. Are instructions given to workers not to lift certain loads without help or supervision?		
6. In the normal working environment, is good posture used?		
7. Is there ample space to allow good posture?		
8. Is the floor and walk area of good quality?		
9. Is the floor and work surface level?		
10. Is the working temperature reasonable?		
11. Is the lighting level sufficient?		
12. Is the air movement reasonable?		

What, in your opinion, are the three most important points to consider for this assessment?

1.
2.
3.

HAZARDOUS SUBSTANCES QUESTIONNAIRE

Respond to these questions, keeping your place of work in mind, and complete as accurately and fully as possible.

	Y/N	Notes
1. Have all hazardous substances stored or used on the premises been listed and COSHH data sheets obtained?		
2. Has the use of each substance been considered as essential? Are safer alternatives available?		
3. Have all necessary safety precautions been established for each hazardous substance?		
4. Are all correct hazard warning signs in place close to the substances in use?		
5. Are all vessels, bags and wrappings that contain hazardous substances clearly marked for the substance stored?		
6. Are all necessary antidotes or neutralizing agents available in close proximity to the hazardous substance?		
7. Is all necessary personal protective equipment/clothing available to all workers who use or come into contact with a hazardous substance? Is it worn and used correctly at all times?		
8. Has full information been given to workers on the hazardous substances that they use or come into contact with, and the associated risks?		

What, in your opinion, are the three most important points to consider for this assessment?

> 1.
>
> 2.
>
> 3.

PERSONAL PROTECTIVE EQUIPMENT QUESTIONNAIRE

Respond to these questions, keeping your place of work in mind, and complete as accurately and fully as possible.

	Y/N	Notes
1. Has suitable personal protective equipment been issued to workers who are exposed to conditions that require special work clothing?		
2. Does the personal protective equipment take into account ergonomic requirements?		
3. Is the personal protective equipment capable of fitting the wearer correctly, after adjustment if necessary?		
4. Does the personal protective equipment comply with current UK or EU standards?		
5. If personal protective equipment is not issued on a personal basis, do workers have clear instructions on where to obtain it?		
6. If more than one item of personal protective equipment is to be worn, are the items compatible?		
7. Have workers been instructed to change personal protective equipment that is past its stated life?		

What, in your opinion, are the three most important points to consider for this assessment?

> 1.
>
> 2.
>
> 3.

Appendix
Suggested
Answers to the
Knowledge Tests

Test your knowledge (1): suggested answers

1. A written and formal assessment of what might or could cause harm in your work.

2. To remove hazards wherever possible and reduce the risk of accidents, ill-health or injury occurring.

3. A hazard is a danger, something with the potential to cause harm. A risk is the likelihood of that danger resulting in an accident or injury.

4. Everyone who might be affected.

5. Any three of the following:

   Manual Handling Operations Regulations 1992
   Display Screen Equipment Regulations 1992
   PPE Regulations 1992
   Health and Safety at Work Act 1974
   Electricity at Work Regulations 1989
   COSHH Regulations 1994
   Noise at Work Regulations 1989
   Fire Precautions Act 1971
   Workplace Regulations (Health, Safety and Welfare) 1992
   Management of Health and Safety at Work Regulations 1992
   Provision and Use of Work Equipment Regulations 1992
   Safety Signs and Signals Regulations 1996
   Consultation with Employees Regulations 1996

6. Yes.

7. No, cost, so long as it is reasonable, cannot be used as a justification for not implementing measures arising from a risk assessment.

Test your knowledge (2): suggested answers

1. Answers may include, but are not limited to, the following:

   Reduced risk of accidents
   Drop in the number of accidents and 'near-misses'
   More productive safety measures
   Reduced costs (due to few accidents and less time off through injury)
   Safety officer keeps their job and stays out of prison!

2. Answers may include, but are not limited to, the following:

   Reduced risk of accidents
   Drop in the number of accidents and 'near-misses'
   Greater peace of mind
   Less time off due to injury and ill-health
   Less chance of death or serious injury

3. Student's own answer.

4. Student's own answer.

5. At regular intervals, or whenever something changes that might affect the level of risk – for example, a new employee, changed working pattern and so on. They are often completed annually.

6. The penalties vary according to the severity of the situation or level of disregard for safety measures. They can include fines, suspension of business and the fining and imprisonment of company directors. The most important consequence is that it is

very difficult, in the event of an accident, to prove that reasonable steps were taken if no risk assessment has ever been carried out.

7. They should be a competent person – that is, they should have a good working knowledge of the legislation and the task or work which they are assessing.

8. The introduction of new machinery or equipment or a change in task/work practice that cause new hazards to be introduced.

Test your knowledge (3): suggested answers

1. Health and Safety At Work Act
2. True
3. Perhaps safety is given a lower priority
4. b) 1 600 000
5. c) 2 200 000
6. c) 30 million
7. Manual handling, followed by slips and trips
8. c) 500

HEALTH AND SAFETY WORKBOOKS

The 10 workbooks in the series are:

Fire Safety	0 566 08059 1
Safety for Managers	0 566 08060 5
Personal Protective Equipment	0 566 08061 3
Safe Manual Handling	0 566 08062 1
Environmental Awareness	0 566 08063 X
Display Screen Equipment	0 566 08064 8
Hazardous Substances	0 566 08065 6
Risk Assessment	0 566 08066 4
Safety at Work	0 566 08067 2
Office Safety	0 566 08068 0

Complete sets of all 10 workbooks are available as are multiple copies of each single title. In each case, 10 titles or 10 copies (or multiples of the same) may be purchased for the price of eight.

Print or photocopy masters

A complete set of print or photocopy masters for all 10 workbooks is available with a licence for reproducing the materials for use within your organization.

Customized editions

Customized or badged editions of all 10 workbooks, tailored to the needs of your organization and the house-style of your learning resources, are also available.

For further details of complete sets, multiple copies, photocopy/print masters or customized editions please contact Richard Dowling in the Gower Customer Service Department on 01252 317700.